PERFECT **POPS**

PERFECT

POPS

THE **50** BEST CLASSIC & COOL TREATS

By Charity Ferreira

Photographs by Leigh Beisch

CHRONICLE BOOKS
SAN FRANCISCO

Library of Congress Cataloging-in-Publication
Data available.

ISBN 978-1-4521-0192-7

Manufactured in China

Designed by Emily Dubin
Prop styling by Sara Slavin
Food styling by Dan Becker

10 9 8 7 6 5 4

Chronicle Books LLC
680 Second Street
San Francisco, California 94107
www.chroniclebooks.com

For Sebastian, whose favorite pop is chocolate-raspberry.

Acknowledgments

Big thanks to my editors at Chronicle Books: Amy Treadwell, for her friendship and for keeping our passion for pops alive; and Sarah Billingsley, for her talented help shaping this book. Thanks also to my testers and tasters: Elijah Lajmer, Kate Washington, Michael Ferreira, Sasha, Talia, Sebastian, Toni, Courtney, Sofia, Gavin, Aiden, Abby, and Race. The biggest thank-you of all goes to Dylan, my tireless and amazingly capable kitchen helper: Thank you for your help with this book; it has been so much fun making pops together!

CONTENTS

INTRODUCTION

Pops are some of the most universally beloved and iconic sweet treats around, equally adored by foodies, hipsters, and preschoolers. Pops occupy a sweet spot between modern and old-fashioned, between gourmet and just plain good. Even the fanciest organic pop is essentially simple and fun, evocative for most of us of hot summer days from childhood.

One of the pops I remember best from my youth is the Eskimo Pie. When my brother and I visited our Southern granddad in the summer, he would take us to get the chocolate-covered ice-cream bars on blisteringly hot afternoons. I loved the moment that my teeth broke the crisp chocolate coating, and the race to get just the right ratio of chocolate and ice cream in every bite before the whole thing melted and rolled right off the stick.

In writing this book, I got to reimagine many of the frozen treats I adored as a kid, such as Dreamsicles, striped Missile pops, Fudgsicles, root beer floats, and malted milk shakes. It was a chance to be true to my happy recollection of these flavors and also to improve on history— if you've ever cherished a memory of a favorite (and maybe highly processed) treat from childhood and then tried it as an adult, you know what I mean. The memory can be shockingly different from the reality!

Some of the pops in this book are inspired by the ice-cream truck—my homage to the Fudgsicle, made with bittersweet chocolate and crème fraîche (page 42); Dreamsicles reinvented with passion fruit juice and vanilla bean ice cream (page 71); juicy, vibrantly hued fruit bars consisting of little more than perfectly ripe summer fruit; and of course, the

Eskimo Pie of my past made with ginger ice cream and a bittersweet chocolate shell (page 74). Other pops are influenced by flavors from all over the world. You'll find pops inspired by Mexican *paletas* (page 36) and by the refreshing jewel-toned *agua frescas* served at taquerias. You'll find pops inspired by Vietnamese iced coffee (page 55), sweet New Orleans–style coffee with chicory (page 73), and the soy chai latte at your neighborhood café (page 54); by creamy Italian cannoli filling (page 70), by the ripe pineapple sprinkled with chile and salt sold as street food in Thailand (page 18), and by Indian *kulfi*, a creamy frozen dessert with saffron and pistachios (page 52).

As I worked on this book throughout a summer, my kitchen saw a steady stream of visitors. I live in a neighborhood with lots of school-age kids, and on some days my son would open the front door, stand on the porch, and shout, "Pops are ready!" Even when he didn't, neighborhood kids always stopped in to ask which pops were new, request their favorites, or bring me plums or lemons from their backyards to make into pops. The kids amazed and inspired me with their sensitive palates and their willingness to try new flavors. It was so much fun to see four- and five-year-olds enjoying pops made from sweet corn or strawberries and balsamic vinegar, and to hear twelve-year-old boys discussing whether or not they liked the flavor of *shiso* in the plum pops, or whether the Mexican chocolate pops should have more chile. I hope these are some of the flavors they will remember when they are adults.

TOOLS,
TIPS & TECHNIQUES
FOR PERFECT
POPS

Pops are easy to make and they don't require much equipment. In fact, you can get by using paper cups and wooden sticks for most of the recipes in this book. But try out a few of these practical tools and tips and your pops will be spectacular.

Pop Molds

The many pop molds on the market (for where to buy them, see Resources, page 90) range in shape from rocket ships to shooting stars. All the recipes in this book were tested using standard bar-shaped molds, each of which holds $1/3$ cup pop mixture. The molds are available in sets of eight or ten and are useful for making pops for a family or a crowd.

Feel free to get creative and use other containers as molds. The Prosecco–Rose Petal Pops (page 84) would be nice frozen in the shape of a tall slender glass for example, and the Sweet 100 Gazpacho Pops (page 32) would make a fun appetizer when frozen in shot glasses. Keep in mind that you'll want to get your mouth around the finished pop (so no highball glasses!) and that you'll need a way to hold the stick in place as the mixture freezes. Covering the container with foil and making a small slit with a sharp paring knife for the stick works well.

Sticks

Many molds come with their own plastic sticks, and you can buy wooden pop sticks in kitchenware stores or online. Purchase more than you think you'll need; they're inexpensive and easy to store, and it's good to have them on hand for spontaneous pop making.

If you have the kind of pop molds that come with a metal cover, it's important to insert the sticks as straight as possible. If they freeze askew, you'll have trouble removing the cover. Wooden sticks tend to float off center in thin pop mixtures. You can get around this problem by soaking the sticks in water first or by straightening them as the pops freeze. Or you can forgo the metal cover and use a piece of foil with slits cut for the sticks. This way, even if the sticks freeze a little crookedly, you'll still be able to remove the cover easily.

Other Tools

Next to pop molds, probably the most useful tool to have is a good blender with a powerful motor that can make short work of puréeing fruits and other ingredients into mixtures for filling the molds. It's also helpful to have a sharp chef's knife for chopping nuts and chocolate, plus a fine-mesh strainer for making silky-smooth purées. And a food processor, while it generally doesn't purée fruit as smoothly as a blender, is a great tool when you want your mixture to retain a bit of texture.

Advance Preparation

Be sure you have space in the freezer to place your filled pop molds. Set out your molds and sticks before you start preparing the mixture so that they're ready when you are.

Unmolding Your Pops

If you're unmolding a few pops at a time, you can run hot water over the outside of the individual mold, below the rim, for a few seconds. Then tug gently but firmly on each stick to pull out the pop. If you're unmolding a whole batch, fill a large bowl with hot water and submerge the entire mold below the rim for a few seconds.

Storing Your Pops

Pops are best if eaten within about a week of making them, and I recommend keeping them in their molds until just before serving or eating. If you need to make a big batch of pops ahead for a party and therefore need to reuse your pop molds, store each pop in its own waxed paper bag, folded carefully around the pop to ward off ice crystals.

Useful Kitchen Chemistry

Your options for pop flavors are practically limitless, but a few basic principles are helpful to know. Sugar and alcohol inhibit the freezing of a mixture. Imagine the difference between an ice cube and a tube of frozen orange juice concentrate—the former is hard as a rock; the latter is soft and slushy. The difference is due to the sugar content. As a rule, the more sugar a mixture contains, the softer it will freeze. Mixtures that have a higher water content will have an icier texture.

Alcohol also inhibits freezing, which is why that bottle of vodka stays liquid in the freezer. Because of this, there is a limit to how much booze you can add to a pop mixture and still have it freeze solid.

All mixtures will freeze best if they are chilled before being poured into the pop molds and if your freezer is turned to the coldest setting.

Swirls, Stripes, and Mix-Ins

Striped pops look impressive, and they're very easy to make. All you have to do is freeze the different-colored mixtures a layer at a time. For a swirled effect, you can combine two thick mixtures (like puddings) or a liquid and an ice cream, as for the Root Beer Float Pops (page 72) or Orange-Passion Fruit Pops (page 71). The liquid freezes around the ice cream, resulting in pops with creamy streaks.

If you want to incorporate ingredients like toasted nuts, whole berries, chopped chocolate, or candy bits throughout your pop, the pop mixture has to be thick enough that the mix-ins will stay suspended as the pop freezes, rather than sinking to the bottom. Thick milkshake and smoothie mixtures are good for this, as are custard or pudding bases. But thinner mixtures, like teas or juices, aren't—the heavier bits will sink to the bottom of the pop.

To toast nuts, preheat the oven to 325°F. Spread the nuts on a baking sheet and toast lightly, about 10 minutes. Cool and then chop finely.

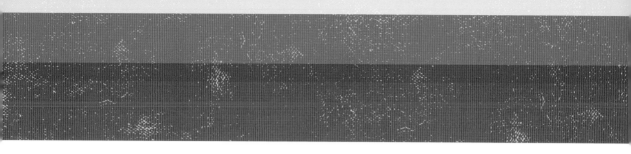

FRUITY POPS

Inspired by juicy Mexican *paletas*, the bright colors and vibrant flavors of the pops in this chapter make them the perfect treat on a hot summer day. Since the main ingredient in these simple, thirst-quenching pops is fresh fruit, it's important to choose the ripest,

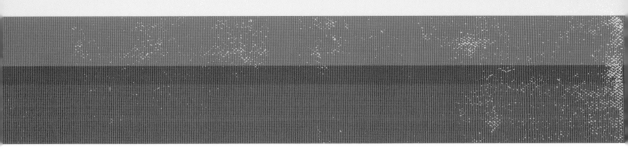

sweetest fruit you can find—delicious fruit will make delicious pops! When strawberries are plentiful at the farmers' market, macerate them with a little sugar and balsamic vinegar and make Balsamic-Strawberry Pops. Celebrate stone fruit season by making Cherry Pops and Plum Pops with Shiso. And, don't forget that tomatoes are fruit, too. The savory Sweet 100 Gazpacho Pops make a great snack or whimsical first course, and are a beautiful way to enjoy colorful heirloom tomatoes.

TUTTI-FRUTTI

A juicy, tangy mixture of red summer fruits, this bright pink pop has a mellow sweetness.

INGREDIENTS

- 1 cup raspberries (about 6 ounces)
- 2 cups hulled strawberries (about 8 ounces)
- 2 cups seeded watermelon cubes (from a 1¼-pound piece)
- 2 tablespoons freshly squeezed lime juice
- ¼ cup sugar

1 In a blender, purée the berries, melon, lime juice, and sugar until very smooth. With a wooden spoon, push the mixture through a fine-mesh strainer into a bowl; discard the solids.

2 Pour the mixture into ice pop molds and insert sticks. Freeze until firm, at least 6 hours or up to 1 week.

3 To unmold the pops, run hot water over the outsides of the molds for a few seconds, then gently pull the sticks.

MAKES **6** TO **8** POPS

LAVENDER LEMONADE POPS

Try selling these at your next lemonade stand! Be sure to use food-safe lavender that hasn't been sprayed with pesticide.

INGREDIENTS

- $2/3$ cup sugar
- $1^1/3$ cups water
- 2 tablespoons packed, fresh lavender blossoms, rinsed
- $2/3$ cup freshly squeezed lemon juice

1 Combine the sugar, $2/3$ cup of the water, and the lavender in a small saucepan. Stir over medium heat until the sugar dissolves and the mixture comes to a simmer. Let stand until cool. Pour the mixture through a fine-mesh strainer into a large bowl. Discard the solids. Whisk in the lemon juice and remaining $2/3$ cup water.

2 Pour the mixture into ice pop molds and insert sticks. Freeze until firm, at least 6 hours or up to 1 week.

3 To unmold the pops, run hot water over the outsides of the molds for a few seconds, then gently pull the sticks.

MAKES **6** TO **8** POPS

PINEAPPLE POPS WITH CHILE & LIME

Pineapples vary a lot in sweetness. If you cut into one and find that it's delicious, that's a great time to make this pop! Cayenne is a hot, red chile pepper. Its firey heat lingers a little and cuts the sweetness of the pineapple.

INGREDIENTS

1	pineapple (about 3½ pounds)
3 to 4	tablespoons sugar
2	tablespoons freshly squeezed lime juice
¼	teaspoon cayenne pepper
	Pinch of salt

1 With a large, sharp knife, cut the top and bottom from the pineapple. Stand the pineapple on a work surface and trim away the rind in strips. Cut the pineapple lengthwise into quarters and trim away the core. Cut the flesh into chunks.

2 Place the pineapple chunks in a food processor and purée until smooth. Transfer to a large bowl and whisk in 3 tablespoons of the sugar and the lime juice, cayenne, and salt. Taste the mixture and add more sugar if necessary.

3 Pour the mixture into ice pop molds and insert sticks. Freeze until firm, at least 6 hours or up to 1 week.

4 To unmold the pops, run hot water over the outsides of the molds for a few seconds, then gently pull the sticks.

MAKES 6 TO 8 POPS

MEXICAN PAPAYA AGUA FRESCA POPS

A touch of honey adds an untraditional but delicious note to this icy thirst-quenching pop. Mexican papayas, which are much larger than the Hawaiian variety, have dense, juicy flesh and a beautiful bright, reddish-orange color.

INGREDIENTS

4 cups cubed Mexican papaya (from about 2 pounds fruit)

½ cup water

3 tablespoons sugar

2 tablespoons honey

1 tablespoon freshly squeezed lime juice

Pinch of salt

1 Place the papaya in a food processor and purée until smooth. Transfer to a large bowl and whisk in the water, sugar, honey, lime juice, and salt.

2 Pour the mixture into ice pop molds and insert sticks. Freeze until firm, at least 6 hours or up to 1 week.

3 To unmold the pops, run hot water over the outsides of the molds for a few seconds, then gently pull the sticks.

MAKES 6 TO 8 POPS

PLUM
POPS WITH
SHISO

Shiso, a member of the mint family, has a delicate flavor that you might recognize from eating the leaves at a sushi bar. If shiso is unavailable, you can make the plum pops without it.

INGREDIENTS

2	pounds red plums
½	cup plus 2 tablespoons sugar
1	tablespoon freshly squeezed lemon juice

8 to 10 fresh shiso leaves

1 Halve, pit, and coarsely chop the plums. In a medium saucepan over low heat, stir the plums, sugar, and lemon juice until the sugar has dissolved and the plum juices are bubbling, 5 to 8 minutes. Let the mixture cool and then transfer to a blender. Add the shiso leaves and purée until smooth.

2 Pour the plum mixture through a fine-mesh strainer into a medium bowl, pressing the pulp with a flexible spatula to extract as much juice as possible. Discard the solids. Pour the mixture into ice pop molds and insert sticks. Freeze until firm, at least 6 hours or up to 1 week.

3 To unmold the pops, run hot water over the outsides of the molds for a few seconds, then gently pull the sticks.

MAKES 8 TO 10 POPS

MELON BLOSSOM POPS

Use the ripest, most fragrant melon you can find for these pops. Cantaloupe and honeydew will work well, as will more unusual varieties like Charentais and Sharlyn. Ask a grower at a farmers' market which melons are the sweetest.

4½ cups peeled, seeded, and cubed melon (from a 3-pound melon)

¼ cup sugar

2 tablespoons freshly squeezed lime juice

2 tablespoons orange flower water

1 In a blender, purée the melon, sugar, lime juice, and orange flower water until very smooth.

2 Pour the mixture into ice pop molds and insert sticks. Freeze until firm, at least 6 hours or up to 1 week.

3 To unmold the pops, run hot water over the outsides of the molds for a few seconds, then gently pull the sticks.

MAKES 6 TO 8 POPS

HIBISCUS-
POMEGRANATE
POPS

This is a contemporary version of the refreshing *agua fresca* called Jamaica, which is made from dried hibiscus flowers. Look for tea that's labeled "pure hibiscus."

INGREDIENTS

2 cups water

2 hibiscus tea bags

1/3 cup sugar

2/3 cup pomegranate juice

1 Bring the water to a boil in a small saucepan. Add the tea bags and let stand for 5 minutes. Remove the tea bags and discard. Whisk in the sugar. Pour into a large bowl and let cool completely. Stir in the pomegranate juice.

2 Pour the mixture into ice pop molds and insert sticks. Freeze until firm, at least 6 hours or up to 1 week.

3 To unmold the pops, run hot water over the outsides of the molds for a few seconds, then gently pull the sticks.

MAKES **6** TO **8** POPS

BLACKBERRY-ICED TEA POPS

This pop tastes like fruit and iced tea, all at once. If you like, add three or four fresh mint leaves to the tea when brewing it.

INGREDIENTS

- 1 cup blackberries (about 6 ounces)
- 2 cups strong black tea, such as Darjeeling or Earl Grey, cooled
- 5 tablespoons sugar
- 1½ teaspoons freshly squeezed lemon juice

1 In a blender, purée the blackberries until smooth. Pour through a fine-mesh strainer into a large bowl, pressing the pulp with a flexible spatula to extract as much juice as possible. Discard the solids. Whisk in the tea, sugar, and lemon juice until well combined.

2 Pour the mixture into ice pop molds and insert sticks. Freeze until firm, at least 6 hours or up to 1 week.

3 To unmold the pops, run hot water over the outsides of the molds for a few seconds, then gently pull the sticks.

MAKES **6** TO **8** POPS

BALSAMIC-
STRAWBERRY
POPS

A little balsamic vinegar and a few grinds of black pepper bring out the sweetness of ripe strawberries.

2 cups sliced, hulled strawberries (from about 1 pound berries)

¼ cup sugar

2½ teaspoons good-quality balsamic vinegar

Freshly ground black pepper

1 Place the strawberries and sugar in a food processor and pulse just until the mixture is finely chopped and juicy but still chunky; you don't want a smooth purée. Transfer to a bowl and stir in the balsamic vinegar and a few grinds of pepper.

2 Spoon the mixture into ice pop molds and insert sticks. Freeze until firm, at least 6 hours or up to 1 week.

3 To unmold the pops, run hot water over the outsides of the molds for a few seconds, then gently pull the sticks.

MAKES 6 TO 8 POPS

CHERRY

POPS

Believe it or not, you don't need a special gadget to pit cherries. Using a sharp paring knife, cut each cherry in half around the pit and remove the pit. Work over a bowl to catch all the precious juice! How much lime juice you add will depend on how sweet your cherries are, so taste as you go.

INGREDIENTS

4	cups cherries (about 1½ pounds)
⅓	cup sugar
1 to 1½	tablespoons freshly squeezed lime juice

1 Pit the cherries and place in a large bowl. Toss with the sugar and let sit until the cherries release their juice, about 15 minutes. Purée the mixture in a blender or food processor until smooth and then add the lime juice to taste.

2 Pour the mixture into ice pop molds and insert sticks. Freeze until firm, at least 6 hours or up to 1 week.

3 To unmold the pops, run hot water over the outsides of the molds for a few seconds, then gently pull the sticks.

MAKES 6 TO 8 POPS

SWEET 100
GAZPACHO
POPS

This savory pop will be prettiest if you use orange and yellow tomatoes mixed in with the red. If you're making the pops for a grown-up brunch (or as an appetizer for a summer cocktail party), feel free to add a few tablespoons of vodka to the mixture before freezing.

INGREDIENTS

- 1½ cups chopped, seeded heirloom tomatoes (from about 8 ounces of tomatoes)

- 1½ cups Sweet 100 cherry tomatoes (about 8 ounces)

- ¾ cup seasoned tomato juice, such as V8

- ⅓ cup finely chopped, seeded English cucumber

- 1 tablespoon freshly squeezed lime juice

- 2 teaspoons finely minced, seeded jalapeño

  Sea salt

1 Place the chopped tomatoes in a food processor and pulse a few times, just until they're a very coarse, chunky purée. Transfer to a large bowl. Repeat with the cherry tomatoes and add them to the bowl. Stir in the seasoned tomato juice, cucumber, lime juice, and jalapeño. Taste the mixture and add up to ½ teaspoon salt. The saltiness of tomato juices varies, so start sparingly, but you'll definitely want the pop to have a bit of a salty flavor.

2 Spoon the mixture into ice pop molds and insert sticks. Freeze until firm, at least 6 hours or up to 1 week.

3 To unmold the pops, run hot water over the outsides of the molds for a few seconds, then gently pull the sticks.

MAKES **6** TO **8** POPS

CREAMY POPS

From ice-cream bars to milk-shake concoctions, the pops in this chapter are made with something creamy to enhance the flavors of ingredients like fruit, nuts, coffee, and—of course—chocolate. Sour cream turns sweet strawberries into Strawberry Cheese-

cake Pops, while bittersweet chocolate becomes the most sublime fudge pop imaginable with the addition of tangy cultured crème fraîche. Milk gives a creamy texture to cinnamon-spiked Arroz con Leche Pops and Sweet Corn Paletas. Yogurt stars in the simple Tart Yogurt Pops, the tangy Key Lime Pops, and the Mango Lassi Pops. You'll find some nondairy options in this chapter, too, like the coconut-flecked Creamy Coconut Pops and the Soy Chai Latte Pops.

SWEET CORN PALETAS

When fresh corn is abundant and at the height of its sweetness in your area, that's when you should make this pop. If fresh corn is unavailable, frozen corn is a fine substitute. Because corn is frozen when fresh, it's a better alternative than less-than-perfect fresh corn.

INGREDIENTS

2 cups whole milk

⅓ cup sugar

3 cups sweet yellow corn kernels (from about 3 ears) or thawed frozen kernels

Pinch of salt

½ teaspoon vanilla extract

1 In a medium saucepan over low heat, combine the milk and sugar and stir to dissolve the sugar. Add the corn and salt and bring to a gentle simmer. Cook, stirring frequently, until the corn is tender, about 3 minutes for frozen corn or up to 10 minutes for fresh. Let cool slightly.

2 Transfer the mixture to a blender and purée until smooth. Pour through a fine-mesh strainer into a medium bowl, pressing the corn with a flexible spatula to extract as much liquid as possible. Discard the solids. Stir in the vanilla.

3 Pour the mixture into ice pop molds and insert sticks. Freeze until firm, at least 6 hours or up to 1 week.

4 To unmold the pops, run hot water over the outsides of the molds for a few seconds, then gently pull the sticks.

MAKES **6** TO **8** POPS

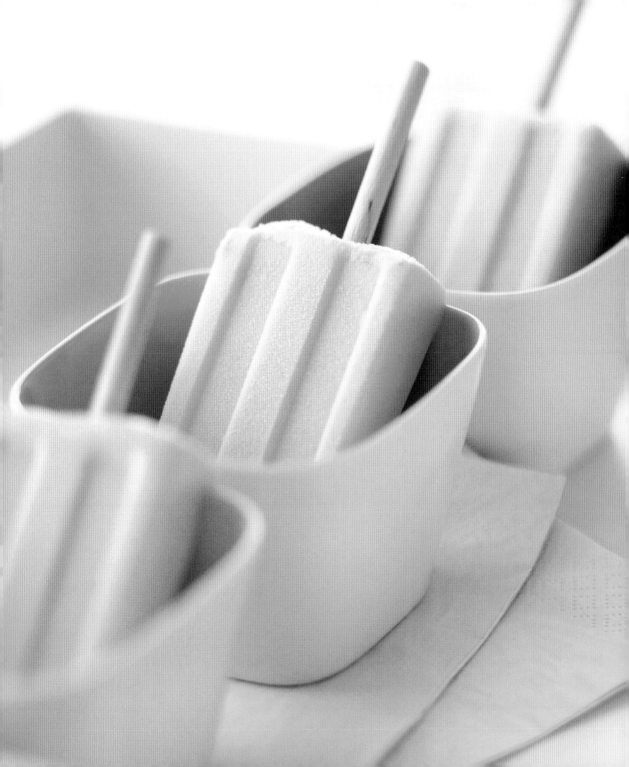

ARROZ
CON LECHE
POPS

Sweet rice cooked in milk is a traditional flavor in Mexican *paletas*. These pops are ultracreamy and spiked with plenty of cinnamon.

INGREDIENTS

2 cups whole milk

¾ cup water

½ cup sugar

½ cup short-grain rice

1 cup heavy cream

½ teaspoon vanilla extract

½ teaspoon ground cinnamon

Pinch of salt

1 In a medium saucepan, stir together the milk, water, and sugar. Stir in the rice and bring to a simmer over medium-high heat. Reduce heat to maintain a simmer and cook, stirring frequently, until the rice is soft but some liquid remains, 20 to 25 minutes. The rice should have the consistency of thin oatmeal. Stir in the cream, vanilla, cinnamon, and salt. Let cool to lukewarm.

2 Pour the mixture into ice pop molds and insert sticks. Freeze until firm, at least 6 hours or up to 1 week.

3 To unmold the pops, run hot water over the outsides of the molds for a few seconds, then gently pull the sticks.

MAKES **8** POPS

DULCE DE LECHE POPS

This is a super-rich, sweet, and milky caramel pop. It has a soft, creamy texture, just like dulce de leche ice cream—it literally melts in your mouth! Baking soda is a traditional ingredient in slow-cooked dulce de leche; it keeps the mixture smooth and gives it its deep, golden brown color.

INGREDIENTS

4 cups whole milk

1 cup sugar

½ teaspoon baking soda

⅔ cup half-and-half

1 In a medium, heavy-bottomed pot over medium heat, combine the milk and sugar and stir until the sugar dissolves and the mixture comes to a simmer. Stir in the baking soda—the mixture will become very foamy at this point—and reduce heat to maintain a gentle simmer. You want to see some bubbling on the surface but not a rolling boil.

2 Cook, stirring the bottom of the pan occasionally with a flexible heatproof spatula to prevent scorching, until the mixture is a deep golden brown and reduced to about 2 cups, 15 to 25 minutes. Let the mixture cool for about 10 minutes. Whisk in the half-and-half and continue to whisk until smooth and well blended.

3 Pour the mixture into ice pop molds and insert sticks. Freeze until firm, at least 6 hours or up to 2 weeks.

4 To unmold the pops, run hot water over the outsides of the molds for a few seconds, then gently tug on sticks.

MAKES **8** POPS

MEXICAN CHOCOLATE POPS

This luscious dark chocolate pop has a hint of texture and spice similar to Mexican ground chocolate.

INGREDIENTS

- **6** ounces bittersweet chocolate, very finely chopped
- **2** tablespoons brown sugar
- **¼** teaspoon ground cinnamon
- **¼** teaspoon cayenne pepper
- **2** cups half-and-half

1 Place the chocolate, brown sugar, cinnamon, and cayenne in a heat-proof bowl. In a small saucepan over medium heat, bring the half-and-half to a simmer. Pour over the chocolate and whisk until the chocolate is melted and the mixture is well combined.

2 Pour the mixture into ice pop molds and insert sticks. Freeze until firm, at least 6 hours or up to 1 week.

3 To unmold the pops, run hot water over the outsides of the molds for a few seconds, then gently pull the sticks.

MAKES **6** TO **8** POPS

CHOCOLATE-CRÈME FRAÎCHE POPS

This chocolate lover's ultimate pop is unlike any other fudge pop you've ever tasted. Be sure to use good chocolate. Trust me—you won't be sorry.

INGREDIENTS

- 2 **tablespoons sugar**
- 2 **tablespoons cocoa powder**
- 4 **ounces bittersweet chocolate, very finely chopped**
- 1 **cup half-and-half**
- 1 **cup crème fraîche (about 8 ounces)**

1 In a large, heatproof bowl, mix the sugar and cocoa powder until no lumps remain. Add the chopped chocolate. In a small saucepan over medium heat, bring the half-and-half to a simmer. Pour over the chocolate mixture and whisk until the chocolate is melted and the mixture is well combined. Whisk in the crème fraîche.

2 Spoon the mixture into ice pop molds and insert sticks. Freeze until firm, at least 6 hours or up to 1 week.

3 To unmold the pops, run hot water over the outsides of the molds for a few seconds, then gently pull the sticks.

MAKES **6** TO **8** POPS

CHOCOLATE-

RASPBERRY
POPS

My son Dylan came up with the recipe for this amazing pop. It tastes like tart raspberry sorbet with a dark chocolate edge. The frozen raspberries give the finished pop a creamy texture.

INGREDIENTS

2 cups frozen raspberries

½ cup vanilla whole-milk yogurt

½ cup whole milk

¼ cup chocolate syrup

1 In a blender, purée the raspberries, yogurt, milk, and chocolate syrup until smooth.

2 Spoon the mixture into ice pop molds and insert sticks. Freeze until firm, at least 6 hours or up to 1 week.

3 To unmold the pops, run hot water over the outsides of the molds for a few seconds, then gently pull the sticks.

MAKES **6** POPS

COOKIES
& CREAM
POPS

I don't know why adding your own choc-olate cookie wafers to vanilla ice cream tastes so much better than buying the ice cream that way. But it does! Nabisco makes a simple chocolate wafer cookie that is perfect in this recipe.

INGREDIENTS

- 1 **pint premium vanilla ice cream**
- 2/3 **cup whole milk**
- 1 **cup crushed chocolate wafer cookies (from about 3 ounces cookies)**

1 Scoop the ice cream into a blender and add the milk. Blend until the mixture has the consistency of a thick milk shake. Stir in the crushed cookies.

2 Spoon the mixture into ice pop molds. You can rap the molds firmly on the counter a few times to settle any air pockets. Insert sticks. Freeze until firm, at least 6 hours or up to 1 week.

3 To unmold the pops, run hot water over the outsides of the molds for a few seconds, then gently pull the sticks.

MAKES 6 TO 8 POPS

BANANA MALTED MILK-SHAKE POPS

This supercreamy malted milk shake has a surprise—banana. The challenge in making this pop is not drinking the milk-shake mixture before freezing it in the molds.

INGREDIENTS

½ to ¾	pint premium vanilla ice cream
1	ripe banana, peeled
3	tablespoons malted milk powder
½	cup whole milk

1 Scoop ½ pint of the ice cream into a blender. Add the banana, breaking it into chunks. Add the milk powder and milk. Blend until the mixture is thick and creamy. Add more ice cream if you prefer a thick shake.

2 Spoon the mixture into ice pop molds. You can rap the molds firmly on the counter a few times to settle any air pockets. Insert sticks. Freeze until firm, at least 6 hours or up to 1 week.

3 To unmold the pops, run hot water over the outsides of the molds for a few seconds, then gently pull the sticks.

MAKES 6 TO 8 POPS

Variation: To make chocolate-banana pops, add ¼ cup chocolate syrup when blending the banana mixture.

STRAWBERRY CHEESECAKE POPS

This sweet, tangy pop has it all, right down to the graham cracker crust.

INGREDIENTS

- 2 cups hulled strawberries (about 8 ounces), plus 6 thinly sliced strawberry wheels (optional)
- ½ cup sour cream
- ¼ cup sugar
- 2 teaspoons freshly squeezed lemon juice
- ½ teaspoon vanilla extract
- ¼ cup coarse graham cracker crumbs (from about 2 crushed crackers), plus more for garnish (optional)

1 Place the hulled strawberries in a blender and purée until smooth. Pour through a fine-mesh strainer into a large bowl, pressing the pulp with a flexible spatula to extract as much juice as possible. Discard the solids. Whisk in the sour cream, sugar, lemon juice, and vanilla. Stir in the ¼ cup graham cracker crumbs.

2 Spoon the mixture into ice pop molds. Slide in the strawberry slices (if using) and insert sticks. Sprinkle crumbs around the base of each pop for garnish, if desired. Freeze until firm, at least 6 hours or up to 1 week.

3 To unmold the pops, run hot water over the outsides of the molds for a few seconds, then gently pull the sticks.

MAKES **6** POPS

MANGO LASSI POPS

This pop is inspired by sweet, cooling *lassi*—my favorite drink to have with Indian food.

2½   **cups cubed mango (from about 1 pound of fruit)**

¾   **cup plain whole-milk yogurt**

¼   **cup sugar**

1 to 2   **teaspoons freshly squeezed lime juice**

¼   **teaspoon ground cardamom**

6 to 8 thinly sliced lime wheels (optional)

1 In a blender, purée the mango, yogurt, sugar, 1 teaspoon of the lime juice, and the cardamom until smooth and creamy. Taste and add more lime juice if desired.

2 Spoon the mixture into ice pop molds. Slide in the lime slices (if using) and insert sticks. Freeze until firm, at least 6 hours or up to 1 week.

3 To unmold the pops, run hot water over the outsides of the molds for a few seconds, then gently pull the sticks.

MAKES **6** TO **8** POPS

CREAMY COCONUT POPS

Coconut lovers, take note! This pop couldn't be simpler—or more satisfying.

INGREDIENTS

One 14-ounce can light coconut milk

¼ cup sugar

¼ teaspoon vanilla extract

   Pinch of sea salt

1 cup sweetened flaked coconut, chopped

1 In a large bowl, whisk together the coconut milk, sugar, vanilla, and salt until well blended. Whisk in the flaked coconut.

2 Pour the mixture into ice pop molds and insert sticks. Freeze until firm, at least 6 hours or up to 1 week.

3 To unmold the pops, run hot water over the outsides of the molds for a few seconds, then gently pull the sticks.

MAKES **6** POPS

KEY LIME

POPS

Key limes are small and round and have a much stronger, dimensional tartness than regular limes. You can sometimes find them in Mexican markets, and you can buy bottled key lime juice at many supermarkets. Pucker up!

INGREDIENTS

2 cups vanilla whole-milk yogurt

⅓ cup sugar

5 tablespoons key lime juice

1 In a large bowl, whisk together the yogurt, sugar, and lime juice until well blended.

2 Pour the mixture into ice pop molds and insert sticks. Freeze until firm, at least 6 hours or up to 1 week.

3 To unmold the pops, run hot water over the outsides of the molds for a few seconds, then gently tug on sticks.

MAKES **8** POPS

PISTACHIO- SAFFRON POPS

Perfect pistachio ice cream should be rich, nutty, and a tiny bit salty. This pop is all that, and more.

INGREDIENTS

1	cup whole milk
1	cup heavy cream
½	cup sugar
1	teaspoon minced orange zest
¼	teaspoon saffron threads
½	cup unsalted pistachios (about 4 ounces), toasted and chopped (see page 12)
2	egg yolks
½	teaspoon vanilla extract
	Pinch of sea salt
6 to 8	thin orange slices (optional)

1 In a medium saucepan, combine the milk, cream, sugar, orange zest, saffron, and pistachios. Bring to a simmer over medium heat, stirring to dissolve the sugar. Remove from the heat, cover, and let stand for 1 hour to infuse the milk with flavor.

2 In a small bowl, beat the egg yolks lightly to blend. Whisk ½ cup of the warm milk mixture into the yolks. Pour the egg yolk mixture into the saucepan. Place over low heat and cook, stirring constantly, until the custard thickens just enough to lightly coat the back of a spoon. Do not let it boil. Remove from the heat and stir in the vanilla and salt.

3 Refrigerate the custard or place in an ice bath and let cool. Cover with plastic wrap, pressing the wrap to the surface to keep a skin from forming. Refrigerate until very cold, at least 4 hours or up to 1 day.

4 Pour the mixture into ice pop molds. Slide in the orange slices (if using) and insert sticks. Freeze until firm, at least 6 hours or up to 1 week.

5 To unmold the pops, run hot water over the outsides of the molds for a few seconds, then gently pull the sticks.

MAKES **6** TO **8** POPS

SOY CHAI LATTE POPS

If you like, you can substitute half-and-half for the soy milk.

INGREDIENTS

- 2 **cups water**
- 6 **green cardamom pods**
- 6 **whole cloves**
- One **1-inch piece fresh ginger, peeled and thinly sliced**
- 4 **black peppercorns**
- 1 **cinnamon stick**
- 2 **black tea bags, such as Darjeeling or Assam**
- ¼ **cup sugar**
- ¼ **teaspoon vanilla extract**
- ⅓ **cup plain soy milk**

1 Bring the water to a boil in a medium saucepan. Remove from the heat, add the spices, and let steep for 10 minutes. Bring to a simmer over medium-high heat, add the tea bags, and stir in the sugar. Let the mixture stand for 10 minutes. Pour the mixture through a fine-mesh strainer into a medium bowl. Discard the solids. Stir in the vanilla and soy milk.

2 Pour the mixture into ice pop molds and insert sticks. Freeze until firm, at least 6 hours or up to 1 week.

3 To unmold the pops, run hot water over the outsides of the molds for a few seconds, then gently pull the sticks to remove.

MAKES 6 TO 8 POPS

VIETNAMESE
ICED COFFEE
POPS

This sweet, icy bar is a frozen version of Vietnamese and Thai iced coffee drinks, both of which feature strong coffee that is flavored with sweetened condensed milk.

INGREDIENTS

2 cups strong coffee, chilled

2/3 cup sweetened condensed milk

1 In a bowl, whisk together the coffee and condensed milk until well blended.

2 Pour the mixture into ice pop molds and insert sticks. Freeze until firm, at least 6 hours or up to 1 week.

3 To unmold the pops, run hot water over the outsides of the molds for a few seconds, then gently pull the sticks.

MAKES **8** POPS

TART YOGURT POPS

If you always choose the "tart" flavor at your neighborhood frozen yogurt shop, this pop is for you. The yogurt is what matters, so choose a good, preferably organic brand like Straus or Ronnybrook. Don't use Greek or "European-style" strained yogurt for this recipe.

INGREDIENTS

2 **cups plain whole-milk yogurt**

⅓ **cup buttermilk**

¼ **cup sugar**

1 In a large bowl, whisk together the yogurt, buttermilk, and sugar.

2 Pour the mixture into ice pop molds and insert sticks. Freeze until firm, at least 6 hours or up to 1 week.

3 To unmold the pops, run hot water over the outsides of the molds for a few seconds, then gently pull the sticks.

MAKES **6** TO **8** POPS

FANCY POPS

Swirls, layers, and stripes—oh my! The pops in this chapter are meant to wow, but the techniques for making them are deceptively simple. Creating colorful striped pops is as easy as freezing the layers one by one, as for the Neo-Neapolitan Pops and the bright pink-and-orange Striped Juice Bar Pops. In

some cases, it's even easier, as for the Raspberry-Vanilla Parfait Pops, in which yogurt and puréed raspberries are simply spooned into the molds and frozen. Good-quality store-bought vanilla ice cream stars in several pops, as a sweet and creamy contrast to strong coffee, root beer, and tart passion fruit. For chocolate lovers, the instructions for Chocolate-Covered Ginger Ice Cream Pops will walk you through the process of enrobing the pops in a crisp shell of bittersweet chocolate. Experiment with color and flavor combinations to create your own spectacular pops.

STRIPED JUICE BAR POPS

This pop will remind you of a drink from your neighborhood juice bar. I came up with this combination for a party celebrating the birthday of a friend's daughter. My friend likes to give her kids healthful sweets, and this pop was a natural. (It is also her daughter's favorite color scheme.)

INGREDIENTS

watermelon-beet juice

2½ cups seeded watermelon cubes (from 1½ pound piece)

2 tablespoons beet juice

2 tablespoons freshly squeezed lime juice

2 teaspoons agave sweetener

carrot-apple juice

1 cup carrot juice

½ cup apple juice

2 tablespoons freshly squeezed lime juice

2 teaspoons agave sweetener

1 To make the watermelon-beet juice: Place the watermelon in a blender and process until liquefied. Pour through a fine-mesh strainer into a small bowl, pressing the pulp with a flexible spatula to extract as much juice as possible. Discard the solids. You should have about 1 cup watermelon juice. Stir in the beet juice, lime juice, and agave sweetener.

2 To make the carrot-apple juice: In another small bowl, stir together the carrot juice, apple juice, lime juice, and agave sweetener.

3 Using a small measuring cup with a pour spout, fill each ice pop mold about one-fourth full with the watermelon juice mixture. Freeze until set, about 30 minutes. Fill each mold another quarter of the way full with the carrot juice mixture. Return molds to the freezer and freeze until set, 30 to 45 minutes. Insert sticks and repeat once more with each juice mixture to make four layers total. Freeze until firm, at least 6 hours or up to 1 week.

4 To unmold the pops, run hot water over the outsides of the molds for a few seconds, then gently pull the sticks.

MAKES 6 POPS

TRIPLE-LAYERED ROCKET POPS

This pop, made with fruit and yogurt frozen in racy stripes, is a big hit with the outer-space set.

INGREDIENTS

1 cup blueberries (about 6 ounces)

4 teaspoons sugar

1 cup vanilla low-fat or whole-milk yogurt

1 cup raspberries (about 6 ounces)

1 Purée the blueberries in a food processor until smooth. With a wooden spoon, press the mixture through a fine-mesh strainer into a bowl, extracting as much juice as possible. Discard the solids. Whisk in 2 teaspoons of the sugar and 2 tablespoons of the yogurt until well combined. Spoon the mixture into ice pop molds, dividing it evenly to fill each mold about one-third full. Freeze for 30 to 45 minutes until set.

2 Divide ⅔ cup yogurt evenly among the molds, placing it on top of the blueberry layer and filling each mold another third of the way full. Freeze until the yogurt layer is set, 30 to 45 minutes.

3 Purée the raspberries in the food processor until smooth. With a wooden spoon, press the mixture through a fine-mesh strainer into a bowl, extracting as much juice as possible. Discard the solids. Whisk the remaining sugar and yogurt into the raspberry purée until well combined. Carefully spoon the raspberry mixture on top of the yogurt layer, dividing it evenly. Insert sticks. Freeze until firm, at least 4 hours or up to 1 week.

4 To unmold the pops, run hot water over the outsides of the molds for a few seconds, then gently pull the sticks.

MAKES **6** POPS

NEO-
NEAPOLITAN
POPS

This pretty layered pop is a frozen yogurt version of that time-honored combination of chocolate, strawberry, and vanilla.

INGREDIENTS

1¼ **cups vanilla low-fat or whole-milk yogurt**

3 **tablespoons chocolate syrup**

1 **cup sliced, hulled strawberries (from about 8 ounces berries)**

1 **tablespoon sugar**

1 In a glass measuring cup or small bowl, stir together ½ cup of the yogurt and the chocolate syrup. Spoon the mixture into ice pop molds, dividing it evenly to fill each mold about one-third full. Freeze for 30 to 45 minutes until set.

2 Divide ⅔ cup yogurt evenly among the molds on top of the chocolate layer. Insert sticks. Freeze for 30 to 45 minutes, until set.

3 Purée the strawberries in a food processor until smooth. With a wooden spoon push the mixture through a fine-mesh strainer into a bowl, extracting as much juice as possible. Discard the solids. Whisk in the sugar and 2 tablespoons of the yogurt until well combined. Spoon the mixture evenly among the molds, on top of the yogurt layer. Freeze until firm, at least 4 hours or up to 1 week.

4 To unmold the pops, run hot water over the outsides of the molds for a few seconds, then gently pull the sticks.

MAKES 6 POPS

RASPBERRY-
VANILLA
PARFAIT
POPS

Because puréed frozen raspberries and yogurt both have thick, creamy textures, you can spoon them into pop molds one after the other for a striking layered effect without taking the time to freeze the layers separately.

INGREDIENTS

1½ **cups frozen raspberries, plus
4 raspberries, halved (optional)**

5 **tablespoons sugar**

1½ **cups vanilla low-fat or whole-milk yogurt**

1 In a blender, purée the 1½ cups raspberries, the sugar, and ½ cup yogurt until smooth and thick.

2 Divide about half of the raspberry mixture equally among ice pop molds. Divide the remaining 1 cup yogurt among the molds. Slide in the halved raspberries (if using). Follow with the remaining raspberry mixture, and insert sticks. Freeze until firm, at least 6 hours or up to 1 week.

3 To unmold the pops, run hot water over the outsides of the molds for a few seconds, then gently pull the sticks.

MAKES 8 POPS

CHOCOLATE-
VANILLA
PUDDING
SWIRL POPS

This is one of my all-time favorite pops. Who doesn't love frozen pudding on a stick?

INGREDIENTS

2 **cups whole milk**

2 **egg yolks**

5 **tablespoons sugar**

2 **tablespoons cornstarch**

Pinch of salt

2 **ounces bittersweet chocolate, finely chopped**

½ **teaspoon vanilla extract**

1 In a medium saucepan, whisk together the milk and egg yolks. In a small bowl, stir together the sugar, cornstarch, and salt. Whisk the sugar mixture into milk mixture. Bring to a simmer over medium heat, stirring constantly with a flexible spatula or a wooden spoon, 4 to 6 minutes. When the mixture starts to bubble around the edges, cook it gently, stirring constantly, for 1 minute. Immediately divide the pudding between two heatproof bowls.

2 Stir the chocolate into one bowl until it is melted and smooth. Stir the vanilla into the other portion. Let the pudding cool to room temperature for about 15 minutes.

3 Spoon the two flavors alternately into ice pop molds, beginning with the chocolate. You can rap the molds firmly on the counter a few times to settle any air pockets. Insert sticks. Freeze until firm, at least 6 hours or up to 1 week.

4 To unmold the pops, run hot water over the outsides of the molds for a few seconds, then gently pull the sticks.

MAKES **6** TO **8** POPS

Variation: For plain vanilla pudding pops, omit the chocolate and increase the vanilla to 1 teaspoon. Skip the step of dividing the mixture in half. For chocolate pudding pops, increase the chocolate to 4 ounces and omit the vanilla.

RICOTTA-RASPBERRY POPS

Sweet, fresh ricotta makes a great pop—it tastes like frozen cannoli filling on a stick. You can substitute 1 teaspoon vanilla extract for the amaretto if you like.

INGREDIENTS

- 1 **cup raspberries (about 6 ounces)**
- 6 **tablespoons sugar**
- 1 **cup whole-milk ricotta**
- 1 **tablespoon amaretto liqueur**
- 1 **teaspoon minced orange zest**
- ¼ **cup finely chopped bittersweet chocolate (about 1 ounce)**
- 1 **cup heavy cream**

1 In a small bowl, mash the raspberries slightly and sprinkle with 2 tablespoons of the sugar. In a large bowl, mix the ricotta with the remaining 4 tablespoons sugar, the amaretto, and orange zest. Fold in the chocolate.

2 In a bowl, whip the cream just to soft peaks. Fold into the ricotta mixture. Gently fold in the raspberries and their juices; avoid overmixing, as it's nice to leave some streaks from the juice.

3 Spoon the mixture into ice pop molds. You can run a knife blade through the mixture to settle any air pockets. Insert sticks. Freeze until firm, at least 6 hours or up to 1 week.

4 To unmold the pops, run hot water over the outsides of the molds for a few seconds, then gently pull the sticks.

MAKES **6** TO **8** POPS

ORANGE-
PASSION FRUIT
POPS

This pop combines sweet-tart passion fruit with streaks of vanilla ice cream flecked with vanilla bean. Frozen passion fruit concentrate mixed with water is an alternative to the juice. Look for it in markets like Whole Foods.

INGREDIENTS

- ¾ cup freshly squeezed orange juice
- ½ cup passion fruit juice or ¼ cup passion fruit concentrate mixed with ¼ cup water
- ⅓ cup sugar
- 1 pint premium vanilla bean ice cream

1 In a large bowl, whisk together the orange juice, passion fruit juice, and sugar until the sugar dissolves and the mixture is well blended. Transfer the mixture to a large glass measuring cup with a pour spout. Refrigerate for at least 1 hour.

2 Use a spoon to fill the ice pop molds loosely with small chunks of ice cream. Work quickly so that the ice cream doesn't melt. You want streaks and chunks of ice cream in the pops rather than for everything to blend together. Avoid packing the molds too tightly; the juice mixture will fill in the space around the ice cream.

3 Carefully pour the juice mixture into a corner of each mold, filling it to the top. Depending on how tightly you fill the molds with ice cream, you'll probably use 1 cup of the juice mixture and almost all of the ice cream. Insert sticks. Freeze until firm, at least 6 hours or up to 1 week.

4 To unmold the pops, run hot water over the outsides of the molds for a few seconds, then gently pull the sticks.

MAKES **8** POPS

FLOAT POPS

Use flat root beer for this pop. If the root beer still has bubbles, it will foam up when poured over the ice cream. Open a bottle or can and leave it in the refrigerator for a day before you plan to make the pops.

INGREDIENTS

  1 **pint premium vanilla ice cream**

1¼ **cups cold, flat root beer**

1 Use a spoon to fill the ice pop molds loosely with small chunks of ice cream. Work quickly so that the ice cream doesn't melt. You want streaks and chunks of ice cream in the pops rather than for everything to blend together. Avoid packing the molds too tightly; the root beer will fill in the space around the ice cream.

2 Carefully pour the root beer into a corner of each mold, filling it to the top. Depending on how tightly you fill the molds with ice cream, you'll probably use about 1 cup of the root beer and almost all of the ice cream. Insert sticks. Freeze until firm, at least 6 hours or up to 1 week.

3 To unmold the pops, run hot water over the outsides of the molds for a few seconds, then gently pull the sticks.

MAKES 8 POPS

Variation: For Cherry Cola Float Pops, substitute cold, flat cherry cola for the root beer. For Purple Cow Pops, substitute cold Concord grape juice.

NEW ORLEANS-STYLE COFFEE & CREAM POPS

Blue Bottle Coffee in Oakland, California, makes a delicious New Orleans-style iced coffee. The sweet, strong coffee is flavored with chicory and plenty of cream. Luckily, you can find Café du Monde chicory coffee in many grocery stores. This pop has streaks of vanilla ice cream to offset the slightly bitter flavor of the coffee.

INGREDIENTS

- 1¼ **cups dark, strong coffee, brewed from a blend of coffee and chicory**
- 2 **tablespoons sugar**
- 1 **pint premium vanilla ice cream**

1 While the coffee is still hot, pour it into a large glass measuring cup. Stir in the sugar and refrigerate until cold.

2 Use a spoon to fill the ice pop molds loosely with small chunks of ice cream. Work quickly so that the ice cream doesn't melt. You want streaks and chunks of ice cream in the pops rather than for everything to blend together. Avoid packing the molds too tightly; the coffee will fill in the space around the ice cream.

3 Carefully pour the cold coffee into a corner of each mold, filling it to the top. Depending on how tightly you fill the molds with ice cream, you'll probably use about 1 cup of the coffee and almost all of the ice cream. Insert sticks. Freeze until firm, at least 6 hours or up to 1 week.

4 To unmold the pops, run hot water over the outsides of the molds for a few seconds, then gently pull the sticks.

MAKES **8 POPS**

CHOCOLATE-COVERED GINGER ICE CREAM POPS

This combination of creamy ginger ice cream and bittersweet chocolate is sublime. Coconut oil is a solid vegetable fat that allows the chocolate to form a thin, smooth coating. You can find it at Whole Foods and other natural foods stores. You'll also need a wire rack and a small offset spatula. It's a good idea to read the instructions all the way through before you begin.

INGREDIENTS

- ⅔ cup whole milk
- 1⅓ cups heavy cream
- ⅓ cup sugar
- ¼ cup thinly sliced, peeled fresh ginger
- 2 egg yolks
- ½ teaspoon vanilla extract
- ½ teaspoon freshly squeezed lemon juice
- 1 pound bittersweet chocolate, finely chopped
- 3 tablespoons coconut oil

1 In a medium saucepan, combine the milk, cream, sugar, and ginger. Bring to just below a simmer—the milk mixture will be steaming but not bubbling—over medium heat, stirring to dissolve the sugar. Remove from the heat and let stand for 15 minutes to infuse the cream mixture with flavor.

2 In a small bowl, beat the egg yolks lightly to blend. Whisk ½ cup of the hot cream mixture into the yolks. Pour the egg yolk mixture into the saucepan. Place over low heat and cook, stirring constantly, until the custard thickens just enough to lightly coat the back of a spoon. Do not let it boil. Remove from the heat and pour through a fine-mesh strainer into a medium bowl. Discard the ginger. Refrigerate the custard or place in an ice bath until cold, about 2 hours.

3 Stir the vanilla and lemon juice into the custard. Pour the custard into ice pop molds and insert sticks. Freeze until firm, at least 8 hours and preferably overnight.

4 Generously grease a wire rack. Place the rack on a baking sheet and chill in the freezer. Unmold the pops by running hot water into a large bowl and submerging the molds to just below the rim for a few seconds. Gently pull the sticks to remove the pops and place them on the wire rack in freezer.

(continued)

5 Fill a saucepan with a few inches of water and bring to a simmer. Combine the chocolate and coconut oil in a heatproof bowl that will fit on top of the saucepan without the bottom of the bowl touching the water. Turn off the heat and place the bowl over the hot water. Stir frequently with a flexible spatula so that the chocolate melts evenly. Keep the chocolate warm while you work. You may need to remove the bowl from the heat, reheat the water, and replace the bowl once or twice during the process of coating the pops. The chocolate mixture should stay thin and liquid.

6 Remove the pops from the freezer. Working quickly with one pop at a time, spoon the warm chocolate over the facing side, lifting the pop by the stick and tilting it to let the chocolate roll off and coat the sides evenly. Place each pop on the rack, chocolate-side up, and freeze until the chocolate is hard, 5 to 10 minutes.

7 Have ready a small offset spatula or other thin metal spatula. Remove the baking sheet from the freezer. Again working with one pop at a time, carefully run the spatula underneath the pop to release it from the rack without cracking the chocolate coating. Turn the pop over and spoon the warm chocolate evenly over the other side. Return the pops to the freezer and allow the chocolate to harden.

8 Serve immediately or cover the rack with plastic wrap and store the pops in the freezer for up to 1 day.

MAKES **6** POPS

GROWN-UP POPS

All pops have the power to make adults feel like kids again, but pops like those in this chapter are among the reasons it's good to be a grown-up. These pops are for friends hanging out in the back-yard on hot summer evenings, intim-ate dinners for two, or swanky pop-tail parties; for gatherings that are winding

down or just getting started; and for a little something sweet after the kids are in bed. Get creative with your presentation of these pops, which are inspired by cocktails and after-dinner drinks. Serve the Sangria Pops upside down in wineglasses, sprinkle the Piña Colada Pops with toasted coconut, or freeze the Bourbon-Peach pops in shot glasses. Because they're made with alcohol, most of the pops have a softer texture than others in this book, which means that you should plan to unmold them right before serving.

GRASS-HOPPER POPS

White chocolate and crème de menthe make a silky sweet version of the blended cocktail.

INGREDIENTS

- **4 ounces white chocolate, very finely chopped**
- **1 cup heavy cream**
- **1 cup half-and-half**
- **3 tablespoons crème de menthe**

1 Place the chocolate in a heatproof bowl. In a small saucepan over medium heat, bring the cream to a simmer. Pour the cream over the chocolate and let stand for 1 minute. Whisk until the chocolate is melted and the mixture is well combined. Whisk in the half-and-half and crème de menthe.

2 Pour the mixture into ice pop molds and insert sticks. Freeze until firm, at least 8 hours or up to 1 week.

3 To unmold the pops, run hot water over the outsides of the molds for a few seconds, then gently pull the sticks.

MAKES **6** TO **8** POPS

PIÑA COLADA POPS

Cool and creamy, with a hint of rum, these pops beg to be made at a beach vacation house and eaten outside before dinner.

INGREDIENTS

1¼ **cups pineapple juice**

½ **cup coconut milk**

3 **tablespoons light rum**

3 **tablespoons sugar**

1 In a medium bowl, whisk together the pineapple juice, coconut milk, rum, and sugar until well blended.

2 Pour the mixture into ice pop molds and insert sticks. Freeze until firm, at least 8 hours or up to 1 week.

3 To unmold the pops, run hot water over the outsides of the molds for a few seconds, then gently pull the sticks.

MAKES **4** TO **6** POPS

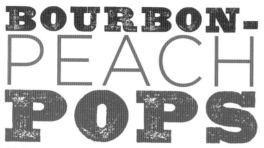

BOURBON-PEACH POPS

Talk about Southern comfort! This boozy, fruity pop will be a big hit at your next summer barbecue. You could purée the peaches in a blender, but hopefully the ones you're using are so ripe you can mash them easily with a fork.

INGREDIENTS

1½ **pounds very ripe yellow peaches (about four medium fruits)**

6 **tablespoons sugar**

2½ **tablespoons bourbon**

1 **tablespoon freshly squeezed lemon juice**

1 Bring a medium saucepan of water to boil. Cut an X on the bottom of each peach. Immerse the peaches in the boiling water for 1 to 2 minutes. Transfer the peaches to a strainer and rinse under cold running water until cool. Starting at the cut end of each peach, slip off the skins.

2 Cut the peaches into chunks and discard the pits. Place the peaches in a large bowl and add 5 tablespoons of the sugar, the bourbon, and lemon juice. Mash with a fork, then switch to a whisk once the mixture turns to liquid. Continue to whisk until the mixture is well combined. Taste and add some or all of the remaining 1 tablespoon sugar.

3 Pour the mixture into ice pop molds and insert sticks. Freeze until firm, at least 6 hours or up to 1 week.

4 To unmold the pops, run hot water over the outsides of the molds for a few seconds, then gently pull the sticks.

MAKES **6** TO **8** POPS

PROSECCO-
ROSE PETAL
POPS

If I were hosting a swanky rooftop engagement party on a hot summer evening, I'd make these refreshing, not-too-sweet ice pops. You'll need to let the Prosecco get flat in the refrigerator before making the pops. If you're in a hurry, decant it into a large bowl, and it will turn flat faster. Be sure to use food-safe rose petals that haven't been sprayed with pesticide.

INGREDIENTS

1 **cup white grape juice**

1 **cup cold, flat Prosecco**

⅓ **cup rose water**

1½ **teaspoons freshly squeezed lemon juice**

About 30 red rosebud petals, rinsed

1 In a large bowl, stir together the grape juice, Prosecco, rose water, and lemon juice. Fill ice pop molds about one-third full. Drop two or three rose petals into each mold and freeze until set, about 30 minutes.

2 Fill the molds another third of the way full and drop two or three more rose petals in each mold. Insert sticks. Freeze until set, about 30 minutes. Fill all the way with the remaining Prosecco mixture and drop two or three more rose petals into each mold. Freeze until set, at least 8 hours or up to 1 week.

3 To unmold the pops, run hot water over the outsides of the molds for a few seconds, then gently pull the sticks.

MAKES 6 POPS

SABAYON
CHIP POPS

Sabayon is an airy, custardy French dessert sauce made with wine and traditionally served with fresh fruit. This creamy pop is a frozen version made with Marsala and shaved bittersweet chocolate—a divine pairing!

Because of the combination of alcohol and the air whipped into the custard, this pop has a soft texture even when completely frozen, so be gentle when unmolding it. Or, for a dinner party, you might freeze the mixture in little dessert glasses, using demitasse spoons for the sticks, and sprinkle extra chocolate shavings over the top. An easy way to make chocolate shavings is by dragging a vegetable peeler across a block of chocolate.

INGREDIENTS

- **4 egg yolks**
- **²/₃ cup sweet marsala**
- **¼ cup sugar**
- **⅛ teaspoon freshly squeezed lemon juice**
- **⅓ cup heavy cream**
- **½ cup shaved bittersweet chocolate (about 1 ounce)**

1 Fill a medium saucepan with several inches of water and bring to a simmer. In a heat-proof bowl that will fit on top of the saucepan (without the bottom of the bowl touching the water), whisk together the egg yolks, marsala, and sugar. Place the bowl over the hot water. Whisk constantly until the mixture becomes thick and foamy, 4 to 5 minutes. Keep an eye on the temperature; if the mixture gets too hot, the eggs will scramble. Whisk in the lemon juice and remove from the heat. Refrigerate the custard until cool.

2 In a large bowl, whip the cream just until slightly thickened. Fold the cream into the chilled custard and then fold in the chocolate. Spoon the mixture into ice pop molds and insert sticks. Freeze until firm, at least 8 hours or up to 1 week.

3 To unmold the pops, run hot water over the outsides of the molds for a few seconds, then gently pull the sticks.

MAKES **6** POPS

NEGRONI POPS

A Negroni is a bright and delicious cocktail of gin, sweet vermouth, and bitters. Campari gives these pretty orange pops a bitter orange flavor and a vibrant color. If kumquats are available, float a few paper-thin slices in the mixture for garnish.

INGREDIENTS

- 2 **cups freshly squeezed orange juice**
- ¼ **cup Campari**
- ¼ **cup sugar**
- 1½ **teaspoons freshly squeezed lime juice**

1 In a large bowl, whisk together the orange juice, Campari, sugar, and lime juice until the sugar is dissolved.

2 Pour the mixture into ice pop molds and insert sticks. Freeze until firm, at least 8 hours or up to 1 week.

3 To unmold the pops, run hot water over the outsides of the molds for a few seconds, then gently pull the sticks.

MAKES 6 TO 8 POPS

SANGRIA POPS

You know how easy sangria is to drink on a hot summer day? These pops go down even easier. If you have enough molds and you're having a party, you might want to make a double batch because they'll go fast. Don't worry about using exceptional wine—an inexpensive red table wine will be fine.

INGREDIENTS

1⅓ cups red wine

1 cup freshly squeezed orange juice

¼ cup sugar

1 tablespoon freshly squeezed lemon juice

1 small orange, peeled and cut crosswise into thin slices

1 In a medium bowl, whisk together the wine, orange juice, sugar, and lemon juice until the sugar is dissolved.

2 Place an orange slice in each ice pop mold. Pour in the sangria and insert sticks. Freeze until firm, at least 8 hours or up to 1 week.

3 To unmold the pops, run hot water over the outsides of the molds for a few seconds, then gently pull the sticks.

MAKES **6 POPS**

CHOCOLATE GUINNESS POPS

The hardest thing about making these pops is not drinking the milk-shake mixture before you spoon it into the molds. Make these pops the next time you invite people over for game night or to watch a soccer match. The famous Irish stout gives good-quality chocolate ice cream a bitter, malty undertone that is irresistible.

INGREDIENTS

1 pint premium chocolate ice cream

¾ cup cold, flat Guinness beer

1 Scoop the ice cream into a blender. Add the Guinness and blend to make a thick milk shake.

2 Spoon the mixture into ice pop molds and insert sticks. Freeze until firm, at least 8 hours or up to 1 week.

3 To unmold the pops, run hot water over the outsides of the molds for a few seconds, then gently pull the sticks.

MAKES 8 POPS

RESOURCES

Amazon
amazon.com
This is the best source for a wide variety of pop molds and wooden sticks in quantities large and small, as well as specialty items like passion fruit juice concentrate, rose water, and key lime juice.

Blue Bottle Coffee
bluebottlecoffee.net
A good mail order source for New Orleans–style coffee blended with chicory.

King Arthur Flour
kingarthurflour.com
A good source for malted milk powder for milkshakes and pops.

Tovolo
tovolo.com
Browse pop molds including rockets, shooting stars, and more, plus ring-gem-pop molds that make frozen jewel-shaped pops to wear on your finger. Note that Tovolo does not sell directly from their Web site; many of their products are available at amazon.com.

Williams Sonoma
williams-sonoma.com
For a variety of pop molds, plus the Zoku Quick Pop Maker, which makes 3 beautiful pops at a time in about 10 minutes.

INDEX

TABLE OF EQUIVALENTS

The exact equivalents in the following tables have been rounded for convenience.

LIQUID/DRY MEASUREMENTS

U.S.		Metric	
¼	teaspoon	1.25	milliliters
½	teaspoon	2.5	milliliters
1	teaspoon	5	milliliters
1	tablespoon (3 teaspoons)	15	milliliters
1	fluid ounce (2 tablespoons)	30	milliliters
¼	cup	60	milliliters
⅓	cup	80	milliliters
½	cup	120	milliliters
1	cup	240	milliliters
1	pint (2 cups)	480	milliliters
1	quart (4 cups, 32 ounces)	960	milliliters
1	gallon (4 quarts)	3.84	liters
1	ounce (by weight)	28	grams
1	pound	448	grams
2.2	pounds	1	kilogram

LENGTHS

U.S.		Metric	
⅛	inch	3	millimeters
¼	inch	6	millimeters
½	inch	12	millimeters
1	inch	2.5	centimeters

OVEN TEMPERATURES

Fahrenheit	Celsius	Gas
250	120	½
275	140	1
300	150	2
325	160	3
350	180	4
375	190	5
400	200	6
425	220	7
450	230	8
475	240	9
500	260	10